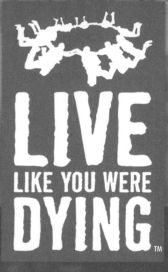

LIVE
LIKE YOU WERE
DYING™

ive Like You Were Dying | Love Deeper | Speak Sweeter | Give Forgiveness | Embrace Eternity

TABLE OF CONTENTS

HOW TO GET THE MOST OUT OF THIS EXPERIENCE

You are about to embark on a life-changing experience in your small group. Studying God's Word together always impacts our lives in powerful and sometimes unpredictable ways. Listed below are the lesson segments for each week as well as some hints for getting the most out of this experience. If you are hosting this group or one of the meetings, refer to the Host Tips and Group Tools in the back of this guide (page 94) for some helpful guidelines for preparing and leading each meeting. An audio training, How to be a Great Host, is included in your church's campaign kit. If you haven't received one of these CDs, ask your church if it is available.

1. **Getting Started:** This fun exercise helps you get to know each other better and begin thinking about the topic of the week. It will be helpful to the group to arrive on time so everyone can benefit from getting to know each other.

2. **Teaching Video:** Watch the ten-minute lesson by relationship expert Gary Smalley and use the study guide to take notes during the session.

3. **Talk It Over:** Discuss five or six questions about the week's topic, and keep these guidelines in mind for participating in a healthy discussion:

   - **Be involved.** Jump in and share your thoughts. Your ideas are important, and your perspective is unique and can benefit the other group members.

   - **Be a good listener.** Value what others are sharing and link what you say to their comments to help the discussion stay cohesive.

   - **Be focused.** Stay on topic. Help the group explore the subject at hand, and try to save unrelated questions or stories for afterwards.

   - **Be careful not to dominate.** Be aware of the amount of talking you are doing in proportion to the rest of the group and make space for others to speak.

   - **Be a learner.** Stay sensitive to what God might be wanting to teach through the lesson as well as through what others have to say.

4. **Live It Out:** Check in with another group member during the week and ask how it's going. Pray for each other. Encourage each other to live out the lessons you are learning in this study. These simple suggestions help the lesson come to life. Don't ignore them; give them a try!

GROUP AGREEMENT

Whenever a new group forms, it is helpful for every member to express what they value in a group, what they expect out of the group, and the commitments they are making to the group. The following Group Agreement is a tool to help you discuss your groups specific guidelines together during your first meeting. Modify anything that does not work for your group, then be sure to discuss the questions that follow. May you have a great group experience!

We agree to the following values:

Clear Purpose To grow healthy spiritual lives by building a healthy small group community

Group Attendance To give priority to the group meeting (call if I am absent or late)

Safe Environment To create a safe place where people can be heard and feel loved (no quick answers, snap judgments, or simple fixes)

Be Confidential To keep anything that is shared strictly confidential and within the group

Spiritual Health To give group members permission to help me live a healthy, balanced spiritual life that is pleasing to God

Welcome Newcomers To invite our friends who might benefit from this study and warmly welcome newcomers

Building Relationships To get to know the other members of the group and pray for them regularly

Other _____

Our Game Plan

- Will we have refreshments? _____
- What will we do about childcare? _____
- What day and time will we meet? _____
- Where will we meet? _____
- How long will we meet each week? _____

FOREWORD

Live like you were dying. A bold concept.

We don't usually like to say the word "dying" in polite conversation. But there it is. We're about to spend thirty days talking about the unspeakable, and hopefully, as we are talking about dying, our living will be transformed.

On our journey together, we'll confront some of the profound thoughts that the writers of the song, "Live Like You Were Dying," penned in their book:[1]

Live like you were dying.

We're all terminal. Some of us are just lucky enough to know it.

Speak sweeter.

Remind your loved ones they are loved. Say it now. Don't wait.

Love deeper.

You can't control the length of your life. Just the depth.

Give forgiveness you've been denying.

Just let it go. And don't forget to forgive yourself.

May we live like we were dying.

*With passion and purpose and mission and meaning…
and with a little wild abandon.
With no forgiveness withheld and no anger held within.*

Our prayer for you is that you embrace the wonderful gift called "life" you have been given. May you learn through this study how to really live your "one and only life" each day for that which is most important.

The Live Like You Were Dying Team

---

1. Tim Nichols and Craig Wiseman, *Live Like You Were Dying*. Thomas Nelson: Nashville, Tenn., 2004. Used by Permission.

LIVE LIKE YOU WERE DYING
DAILY READINGS

By John Fischer

Staring Down Death
Week 1; Day 1

Death is the most inevitable event that we are least prepared for. There is great irony in this in that there is, for each of us, a hundred percent chance of dying and a next to a hundred percent chance we aren't anywhere near ready for it. Our whole culture is in a state of denial when it comes to death.

Our elderly family members die in nursing homes sometimes far removed from the families they nurtured and that nurtured them. We are often not even there when they breathe their last. And the main goal of the funeral home is to shield the family members as much as possible from the reality of what just happened.

But we are embarking on a 30-day journey to change all that.

The Bible clearly states that we all have an appointment with death —*"It is appointed for men to die once and after this comes judgment"* (Hebrews 9:27 NASB). But instead of running from that appointment, as so much in our culture encourages us to do, we are going to run right for it. We are going to fearlessly stare down death and find out what changes when we do. We are going to ride right up to the precipice and let the winds from the valley of death blow back over our lives and stir us to something new.

This study has one goal: Change. We want you to discover

that one thing that will alter the course of your life that you wouldn't find any other way unless you lived like you were dying.

This will take courage, but we have help in this: *"Even though I walk through the valley of the shadow of death, I will fear no evil, for you are with me"* (Psalm 23:4).

We have company.

You see there is no way we could have the nerve to face death — even hypothetically — if we didn't know that the Son of God has already stared down death and won. He's been there and back, and he is going to lead us right up to it, through it, and on to the other side. So what do we have to fear?

We are going to assume that we only have thirty days to live, and reevaluate our values, priorities and dreams in light of that. How would this knowledge change the way you look at things? What might you be emboldened to do that you have never done before? What would become important, and what would suddenly not matter at all? We want to invite you to explore these questions with us on this 30-day journey.

This experience will have different results for each person.

Someone might take that trip they've wanted to take for a long time. Another might learn to paint. Someone might discover the words "I love you" roll more easily off their lips. Someone might reunite a broken relationship through the gift of forgiveness. Others

_____

_____

_____

_____

_____

_____

_____

_____

_____

_____

_____

_____

_____

_____

_____

_____

_____

_____

_____

might talk more freely about Jesus. It's unpredictable what exactly might happen because we're all different and we will all interpret the message in a different way, but that's the beauty of it. It will be your way...how God inspires you. What happens in the next thirty days will be entirely up to you. Are you ready to live like you were dying?

Please read carefully the following declaration and sign it as a symbol of your commitment.

I am willing to do what God wants me to do to act on the insights I receive in the next thirty days, not just think about them. I am willing to take risks I might not normally take unless I knew I was dying soon. I am willing to stare down death and grab a hold of my life.

Signed:

_____

Response

1. What thoughts and emotions come to mind when you think of "death"?

2. In what ways do you feel unprepared for death?

Death, False Alarms and Second Chances
Week 1; Day 2

Have you ever had a false alarm as to the where-abouts of someone you love? It can strike you anytime, like when you hear about an accident on the freeway your spouse takes to work and now can't reach him on his cell phone. Or when your kids are out and sirens sound in your neighborhood. Or your mom goes in for a biopsy and now you are waiting on the results.

For a moment, in situations such as these, you live with the reality that something terribly bad has happened. Perhaps it hasn't — you can't confirm it either way — but your emotions have a tendency to assume the worst, so that at least in the area of your feelings, it's as if it has happened.

The challenging thing is how powerless we are to stop the flow of feelings and "what-ifs" in times like these. It's like trying to shut off a faucet stuck in the "on" position with a broken valve. You can pray, but you can't stop the flood of emotions.

Sometimes this can be good, even though it turns out to be a false alarm. For the moment that we feel this, we experience life from a far different perspective. Suddenly that argument you had with your husband seems so petty. You regret the tone of voice you used to berate your children for not doing their chores. You start searching for the last time you told your mom you loved her and you can't remember.

This is exactly the frame of mind we want to be in for the next few weeks, only we are the ones with the bad news. This may be a false alarm, but we don't really know that for sure, so we are going to live as if we were dying and each day we wake up breathing will be like a second chance.

What would become important if you only had weeks to live? What would not? What will this false alarm do to your relationships and priorities? You have a second chance at life. What will you do?

When the prodigal son returned home after blowing his inheritance, he was greeted with this: "Quick! Bring the best robe and put it on him," exclaimed his father after throwing his arms around his son. *"Put a ring on his finger and sandals on his feet. Bring the fattened calf and kill it. Let's have a feast and celebrate. For this son of mine was dead and is alive again; he was lost and is found"* (Luke 15:22-24).

This father thought his son was dead, but it was a false alarm. For the son it's a second chance and this time he has a much different perspective. He's even willing to be a servant on his father's farm, just to be home. He has a whole new set of priorities now.

What will your priorities be?

Response

1. Have you ever had a false alarm in relation to
   yourself or someone you love? What was it like?

2. As honestly as you can, arrange the following
   categories in order of their current priority, being
   careful to not order them the way you think they
   are supposed to be, but the way they really are in
   your life based on the time and attention you pay
   them: work, God, family, recreation, health,
   friends, ministry.

3. How would you readjust this list if given a
   second chance?

The Time Is Short
Week 1; Day 3

George was a staunch unbeliever. At 55, he found out he only had a short time to live due to pancreatic cancer, a particularly potent form of this dreaded disease. Certain things began to change for George. He slowed down some, let his hair grow, became more frank in his speech (which was already pretty colorful), but he also became more belligerent. These changes did not escape the notice of his neighbor who was a Christian and found it impossible to share anything about salvation or eternity with George without a near violent reaction. George had been angry with God before this happened (he had some understandable reasons to be), but now he was really cantankerous.

Truth of the matter is: none of us has very long to live. It's all relative. Paul calls us to live all the time as if the end is near. Read what he wrote in 1 Corinthians 7:29-31:

"What I mean, brothers, is that the time is short. From now on those who have wives should live as if they had none; those who mourn, as if they did not; those who are happy, as if they were not; those who buy something, as if it were not theirs to keep; those who use the things of the world, as if not engrossed in them. For this world in its present form is passing away."

What he's saying here is that an eternal perspective on your life will govern your emotions and keep you from being defined by your possessions and caught up in the escalating rat race of accumulating more and more. If George had already gained this kind of perspective on life, the news of his terminal condition would have been a lot easier to take. According to Paul, life is already short, and we are better off living with this reality in mind.

Paul would have liked the "Live Like You Were Dying" song. He would say that if you live like you were dying, the following things would be true:

1. You would hold your most precious things loosely — even your spouse.

2. You would find your emotions tied more to God, your hope in Christ and your love for others because these things are eternal.

3. You would realize that when it comes to earthly possessions, you don't really own anything.

4. You would use things to love people, not use people to get more things.

Thankfully, George did finally come around to consider the gospel and accept Christ's free gift of salvation. Fortunately his neighbor ended up taking him to a Willie Nelson concert (George was a huge fan) where an unexpected 20-minute set of gospel songs, all about going home to be with the Lord, got through to him where nothing else could! Maybe Willie knows that time is short too.

Response

1. If you found out today you only had a month to live, what immediate changes would you make? Which of these could you make right now?

2. Do a serious gut-check about what has a hold of your heart. What is one thing you need to let go of today?

3. What is one positive change you could make for your life today?

The Sky Is Talking
Week 1; Day 4

The heavens declare the glory of God; the skies proclaim the work of his hands. Day after day they pour forth speech; night after night they display knowledge. There is no speech or language where their voice is not heard. Their voice goes out into all the earth, their words to the ends of the world. (Psalm 19:1-3)

Shhh...Listen...Hear that? It's the sky talking. And what's it saying? All kinds of stuff about God and everything he's made. It never stops. It's a praise song always playing, but we've gotten used to ignoring it. There is communication and knowledge bound up in the sky, the clouds, and the stars — it's streaming all over the planet 24/7 — and we can learn to tap into it.

God's presence through his creation is something we have probably all felt at one time or another. It might have been a golden sunset, the power of the crashing surf, the wind in the high-mountain trees, or the beauty of a crisp fall morning. Sometimes, it can be so overwhelming you don't know what to do with yourself. But these are usually moments that take us by surprise. We didn't plan on it; the moment captivated us while we were on the way to some-where else.

If you only had a month to live, chances are you would make time to go where you could hear from God through what he has made. Be intentional. Turn the sunset into an event. Take an evening walk with God. Make plans to see natural wonders you've always wanted to see. Take a hike into the wilderness. Walk through a garden. Sit out under the stars one night.

The important thing when you do any of this is to make sure you have plenty of time to just sit and be still. Let everything fade out except what the heavens are declaring. What do you hear? What is God saying about himself through his creation? You have to train yourself to do this. You may not hear anything at first, but don't give up. You have to get used to the silence before you can start to pick up anything. And it's best to do this alone. If you're with others, take off by yourself for a while so you can go at your own pace.

I'm a backpacker, myself, and I notice when I pack into the wilderness with my kids or a friend, the further in we go, the less we seem to talk. Something takes over that makes talk seem cheap — like we're desecrating something sacred. We probably are. We are interrupting the holy dialogue. God was saying something. Hush…now, where were we?

"It is not the number of breaths you take; rather, it is the number of moments that take your breath away that really matter."

Response

1. Where and how do you best hear from God?

2. Make a plan to go to a place where you can spend some uninterrupted time with God. Be sure to allow time to listen, look, and linger.

3. If you only had days to live, what would you want to hear from God? What would you want to ask him?

L'Chaim!
Week 1; Day 5

Jewish tradition has a phrase for living well: "L'Chaim — to life!" The phrase is not to a good life, to a healthy life, or even to a long life. It is simply to life, recognizing that life is indeed good and precious and should always be celebrated and savored. L'Chaim!

All of life is a gift from God.

"Since everything God created is good, we should not reject any of it. We may receive it gladly, with thankful hearts." (1 Timothy 4:4 NLT)

"Whatever is good and perfect comes to us from God above, who created all heaven's lights." (James 1:17 NLT)

The love of life is not in conflict with loving God, because God is the giver of all that is good in life. To enjoy life is to enjoy God as the giver of all good things whether one realizes it or not. A person who doesn't know God — even someone who doesn't believe there is a God — can still love and enjoy life. They just don't know who to thank.

If you knew you had only a short time to live, you would want to especially enjoy those things in life that you love and value the most. And depending on how able you were, you might want to try some of those things you never had a chance to do. (This is where the lyrics from "Live Like You Were Dying" come in…skydiving, rocky mountain climbing, and trying your luck on "Fumanchu"). I know my wife would be on the next plane to Paris, even if it meant hocking everything we have to get there. What about you? What would you do?

Of course, this is what the song, "Live Like You Were Dying," is getting at — a kind of second chance at life. Someone with a relatively healthy life might live longer, and yet never get around to doing half the things they might have done had they known earlier that their life was going to be cut short. This is the advantage to knowing you're terminal — you get more out of life because you better appreciate what you have while you have it. Love is more intense; insight is keener; awareness is heightened; hope is more certain; colors are more vibrant; faith is more real.

A friend of mine named John was paralyzed from the waist down due to a bicycle accident while only in high school. In the first few years he struggled bitterly with why this had happened to him, but then a monumental change took place. He made peace with God and with his condition, and found that his anger was replaced by a zest for life that far eclipsed those with full capacity of their limbs. For one thing, John realized a lifelong dream of being a Christian comedian — he just does it from a wheelchair. Then I found out that he jumped out of a plane with his eighty-three-year-old skydiving grandmother! "L'Chaim!" must run in this family!

Appreciate what you have while you have it. Celebrate life! To the adventure! To risk! To love! To life... L'Chaim!

Response

1. Spend the next few moments thanking God for the gift of life. Think of some of your best "life moments" and express your appreciation to God.

2. What is it you have always wanted to do but never took the chance?

3. What risks might you be willing to take in the next thirty days? Go for it!

The Tongue Is a Fire
Week 2; Day 1

Have you ever had words come out of your mouth that you wished you could take back even as you spoke them? You let your anger get the best of you and yelled at your kid even though you knew you were taking your frustrations out on him. Or you felt trapped in a corner and lashed out at your husband or your roommate. When frustration and anger are held inside, they build in intensity until they have nowhere to go but an explosion at the nearest, often unsuspecting person. It can be your spouse or a total stranger. It can be your dog or cat, for that matter!

The Bible says: *"Consider what a great forest is set on fire by a small spark. The tongue also is a fire, a world of evil among the parts of the body"* (James 3:5-6). Our words can do incredible damage.

They can abuse. They can tear down one's self-esteem. They can drive a knife through someone's heart. Used over and over to wear someone down, they can ruin an entire life.

Words can also do incredible good. They can make a person feel like a million bucks. They can give someone hope. They can give someone courage. They can make someone feel loved and valued. All of this simply by the words we speak.

But words don't come out of a vacuum, either. Jesus taught that what we say begins in the heart.

"The good man brings good things out of the good stored up in his heart, and the evil man brings evil things out of the evil stored up in his heart. For out of the overflow of his heart his mouth speaks." (Luke 6:45)

If we are going to speak sweeter, then the work has to start inside. Bring those angry and hurtful things to the Lord. Get mad at him if you need to; he can handle it. Let him replace negative influences with his love and acceptance. Focus on the fruits of the Spirit which are… *"love, joy, peace, patience, kindness, goodness, faithfulness, gentleness and self-control"* (Galatians 5:22–23). These are the qualities the Spirit of God is already developing in you, and you can call upon them as needed. These are also the qualities that will sweeten your speech.

As you seek to speak sweeter, here are some practical things to help you.

1. Try not to be reactive. Many of our most damaging words come as knee-jerk reactions to being hurt or wounded.

2. Pause… take sixty seconds. *"Everyone should be quick to listen, slow to speak and slow to become angry"* (James 1:19). Learn to think first before you speak. The damage is done when

our emotions take a shortcut by our brain and go straight to our tongue. Practice putting some separation between your emotions and your words. If you need a time out, take it. Time outs aren't just for kids and ball players, you know.

3. Listen, observe, and discover. Find out the words that make those you live with and love feel treasured and valued. Remember, you don't have much time. Say it, instead of wishing you'd said it when it's too late.

Response

1. Do an inventory on the condition of your heart. Besides the fruits of the Spirit listed above, there are what Paul calls *"acts of the sinful nature…hatred, discord, jealousy, fits of rage, selfish ambition, dissensions, factions and envy"* (Galatians 5:14–21). Do any of these words describe what's in your heart? What fruits of the Spirit will best combat them?

2. Talk to your spouse/roommate/family members about establishing a "time out rule." Set some ground rules for it so everyone has permission to use it.

3. Which of the three practical steps in this daily reading is the one you most need to practice?

A Kind Word
Week 2; Day 2

"Kind words are like honey—sweet to the soul and healthy for the body." (Proverbs 16:24 NLT)

My neighbor walked out of her house the other morning looking like she had the world on her shoulders. All the way to her car, her gaze was fixed on the ground and I could see the furrows on her brow from across the street. She was so set on her moody thoughts that she didn't see me pacing in front of my house cooling down from a morning jog. My neighbor does a good deal of traveling, so I really meant it when I yelled over to her, "Hi Doris! It's so nice to see you around these days!"

Well you wouldn't believe the change in countenance that swept instantly over her face. I've never seen anything like it — such a dramatic change. I could almost read her thoughts. It was as if she were saying, "Your words are so much better than what I was just thinking about. I think I'll choose your version of this moment right now over mine!"

We underestimate the difference we can make in someone's life, even a stranger's, with a kind word.

We live such isolated lives these days behind invisible walls. We walk by each other on the street, stand next to each other in the elevator, wash our hands beside each other in the restroom without a word or even an acknowledgment that the other exists. So many people are afraid, trapped in their own private loneliness. This isolation presents an incredible opportunity for those of us who are followers of Christ. There's enough time left to overcome that fear and reach out to someone with a smile and a kind word.

Yes, even a smile can do it. When you smile at someone you are saying, "I see you there. Whoever you are, and whatever you are going through, you are worth noticing." Try it and watch people light up.

John Kevin Hines is one of a handful of people who have survived an attempted suicide jump off the Golden Gate Bridge. He claims to have told himself that if any one of the hundreds of people he rubbed shoulders with on the way to the bridge noticed he was distraught, and asked him what was wrong, he wouldn't jump. That's all it would have taken — another human being to acknowledge his existence. No one did. On his way down he literally got a hold of his life and asked God for a second chance, which is miraculously what he got, or we never would have heard how he was a smile away from death.

It doesn't take much. Just a few simple words to my neighbor that morning actually changed her countenance and outlook. And, I can't help but believe that the smile on her face lasted at least a few blocks down the road. Who knows, it might have just altered her whole day.

Response

1. Think back to an occasion when someone spoke words of encouragement to you just at the time you needed them. What difference did it make in your life?

2. Is there someone you see regularly whose life you could affect by a kind word or two?

3. Make it your goal to make eye contact with people you pass throughout the day and acknowledge their existence. And say a kind word to those you see regularly like store clerks, bank tellers, waiters, or neighbors.

Finding the Words
Week 2; Day 3

What keeps us from saying what we really feel to those we love? If we are afraid, what are we afraid of? What are some of the barriers that keep us from expressing what is really in our hearts? How can we remove them?

I'm sure you know the feeling. The love is there — you may even rehearse what you are going to say — but when you open your mouth in that person's presence something else comes out, or in some cases, nothing at all. You might even notice yourself doing or saying exactly the opposite of what you really want.

We are all victims of the patterns that have formed in our lives and relationships — well-worn grooves into which we fall without trying. And maybe that's part of the problem right there: we aren't trying. These patterns can become so deep, it takes something earth-shattering to force us out of them. This change of perspective is precisely the by-product of living like you were dying.

If you were dying, you would find it easier to say the things you always wanted to say to your loved ones. In the Old Testament, when Jacob was about to die, he called his sons together. *"…these are the blessings with which Jacob blessed his twelve sons. Each received a blessing that was appropriate to him"* (Genesis 49:28 NLT).

What we're talking about doing during these thirty days is changing the lens through which we see people. Don't wait until you are on your deathbed to speak words of blessing.

Here are some ways you might do this. If it's a spouse, remember the one you married — the wife/husband of your youth. Recall why you loved them in the first place and reattach yourself to that love. If it's a child or sibling, remember their best qualities. See them as you would see them from your deathbed and bless them for who they are. If it's a parent, regardless of how they may have failed you, they gave you the gift of life and for that you can be eternally grateful. Remember they have had their own struggles in life, some of which you may never understand, because they lived in a different time and place.

Don't be shy. Speak what's in your heart; this may be your last chance to let someone know. Don't leave your loved ones wondering if you loved them just because you didn't have a chance to tell them. Tell them now.

When it comes to speaking your heart, there is no better time than the present. And if you can't express what you really want to say, try living like you were dying.

Response

1. What are some of your barriers to speaking sweeter to those you love?

2. Ironically we usually experience the greatest barriers to expressing our true feelings with the ones we know the best. Think about that person in light of what you would say to them if you were dying. Write it down if you need to, then commit yourself to saying it soon…TODAY.

3. One of the most powerful ways to speak sweeter is through writing a letter. Consider taking the time to write a "love letter" to somebody you care about deeply.

On-the-spot Praying
Week 2; Day 4

One of the most powerful ways we can "speak sweeter" is praying not only for people but with them. There is nothing quite like the gentle strength of a person praying over you.

Have you ever had someone stop everything and pray for you? You were talking with them on the phone or standing in the parking lot having a conversation and that person sensed something in your voice that said you were particularly worried or stressed, so he or she put a hand on your shoulder and said, "Would you mind if I prayed for you right now?" Suddenly you felt the tension go out of your body, you were flooded with warmth, and the words from that person's mouth flowed like cool water over your thirsty soul. "May I pray for you?" may be some of the sweetest words to come out of someone's mouth. It's not only the prayer; it's the fact that someone cares enough to notice a need and do something about it.

Some Christians have been known to say this to perfect strangers when sensing someone in great distress. Few people, regardless of their beliefs, will turn down prayer, especially in a time of need.

We need to be quicker on the draw when it comes to praying for each other. We need to get more in the habit of praying on the spot for people instead of saying we will pray for them at some time in the future. The latter is a statement of intention, and we all know what can happen to our best intentions. Pray on the spot, because otherwise you might forget; and pray on the spot, because of what your verbal prayer can do for someone in and of itself. If you're on the Internet, type your prayer out and send it.

My mother touched hundreds of people's lives from her breakfast room. She was what some people call a "prayer warrior" and she had a team of other warriors she would call up in severe cases. People would call her and she would always pray for them over the phone. You wouldn't believe the number of people who came forward at her memorial service to remember what those prayers meant to them.

Prayer becomes more essential the nearer we come to the end. Here's what Peter said about it: *"The end of all things is near. Therefore be clear minded and self-controlled so that you can pray"* (1 Peter 4:7). Of all the things he could have said given that the end is near, prayer seems the least likely. Yet it is the first thing he mentions. And notice he doesn't say to pray, but to be continually in a state of mind where you are ready to pray. When you are ready to pray, you are more likely to be on the spot with your prayers. When you're ready to pray, you'll find there are people who need it all around you.

Response

1. Make a list of people you would like to pray for and begin to look for an opportunity to pray for them in person.

2. It's hard to speak ill of someone or gossip about them when you are praying for them. Is there anyone in your life for whom prayer would sweeten the way you speak about them?

3. Read Ephesians 1:14–19 which is a prayer by the Apostle Paul. Notice how different his prayer is than our prayers. Make a list of things he prays for and start praying the same things for your friends.

Say It
Week 2; Day 5

My wife and I were in a meeting with the head of a new tutoring program for our son, along with a supervisor and his tutor who is twentysomething with long black hair and pretty dark eyes. She has taken up a new job on the side as a clothing store manager and significantly upgraded her appearance from when our son started the program. Today, coming straight from work, she was nothing short of stunning.

Our meeting began like a standard business meeting. We all ignored the elephant in the room, which was this woman's sheer beauty, until my wife, never at a loss for words, turned to her and blurted out in the middle of a sentence about something else, "I don't think I've ever told you how absolutely beautiful you are." The tutor flushed while the other two women appeared flustered for a moment, and then the meeting continued on as before yet with a sense of genuine value that had trumped lesser thoughts.

As the truth always does, my wife's acknowledgment cut through whatever inappropriate thoughts or games were going on right then in our minds. My temptation to see my son's tutor as anything other than someone beautiful God created, the other two women's probable jealousy, not to mention my wife's struggle in that same area, all dissipated into sheer appreciation of the truth. It was no big deal. It was just my wife speaking sweeter.

You and I have the power to change someone's life. We can acknowledge the beauty that is there or pull out the beauty that is hidden — the beauty of soul and character where only God looks. *"Man looks at the outward appearance, but the LORD looks at the heart"* (1 Samuel 16:7). We can find the beauty where there is old age, sadness, deformity, or just plain run of the mill drabness. We have the power to make someone better with our words or lesser without them.

My wife's comment was not out of character for her. She does this all the time. It is her gift to encourage and lift up others and I have noticed that people love to be around her as a result. She does this unselfishly, and I marvel at how a person's sense of who they are can blossom around this kind of verbal affirmation. With so much wearing and tearing down in the world, we could all use more lifting up.

The writer of Hebrews says *"But encourage one another daily, as long as it is called Today, so that none of you may be hardened by sin's deceitfulness"* (Hebrews 3:13). We are challenged to encourage "today" because when you think about it, that is really all we have. Yesterday is gone and tomorrow is unknown.

God spoke the world into existence. That's how power-ful words are. If the same God is telling you to say something, you'd better say it. And don't wait. You may not get a chance tomorrow.

Response

1. Think about a time when someone encouraged you by something they said. How did it make you feel? Knowing that, seek to encourage someone every day this week.

2. If someone were to follow you around this week, which would describe you more — critical or complimentary? gracious or grumpy? building up or tearing down?

3. Write down what God is telling you to say to someone, and say it.

What Will Last
Week 3; Day 1

"There are three things that will endure — faith, hope, and love — and the greatest of these is love" (1 Corinthians 13:13 NLT).

When time is running out, the main things suddenly become the main things. The unnecessary falls away. If you knew you were looking forward to eternity with God, you would want to spend your last days focusing on that which would translate from this life to the next. When you think of it, the things that last make up a pretty short list.

When asked to name the greatest commandment in the law, Jesus replied, *"'Love the Lord your God with all your heart and with all your soul and with all your mind.' This is the first and greatest commandment. And the second is like it: 'Love your neighbor as yourself.' All the Law and the Prophets hang on these two commandments"* (Matthew 22:37–40).

What an amazing revelation. There are two things, and only two, we experience now that will carry on into eternity: our relationship with God, and our relationships with one another — and love is the driving force that holds them together. That is all. Love, as the Bible defines

LIVE
LIKE YOU WERE
DYING

it, is truly the greatest thing in the world. Love is of God, and God is love. You can't get any closer to the heart of God.

1 Corinthians 13 defines love for us, and since love is the greatest thing in the world, we should be all over this. Let's take a look.

"Love is patient and kind." Patience gives people time to change. It gives them the benefit of the doubt. When I am impatient with my children, it's because I am thinking of myself first. I have my own agenda they are messing up. This is why kindness is right on the heels of patience: it takes kindness to not act out of your own impatience. By being kind, I am appreciating the value of those around me, and taking their good into consideration.

"Love is not jealous or boastful or proud or rude." All of these ugly things spring from the self. Love does not take its own needs into account, mainly because it has no needs; it is all about giving. Love extends outward toward others, never inward toward self, because it is entirely unselfconscious. It does not *"demand its own way."*

"Love is not irritable, and it keeps no record of when it has been wronged." This is not allowing others to walk all over you, it is merely saying, "Yes, you wronged me — yes, that hurt — but I

am choosing not to hold it against you. In fact, if you bring it up again, I will not know what you are talking about."

"[Love] is never glad about injustice but rejoices whenever the truth wins out." Love is impartial and seeks what is right and just for everyone. Love knows what is right, and does it, even if there is a price to be paid for speaking the truth. And why not, when you're living like you were dying anyway?

Finally, *"love never gives up, never loses faith, is always hopeful, and endures through every circumstance..."* even the ultimate circumstance of death itself. Forget the Energizer Bunny, love just keeps on going.

Response

1. How much do the characteristics of love you just read about define your relationships?

2. Which ones are you doing well in and which ones do you need to pay attention to?

3. Pick one characteristic of love you would like to grow in, then develop a prayer and a plan to see more of it in your life.

Love In Any Language
Week 3; Day 2

"Je t'aime."

"Ich liebe dich."

"Ti amo."

"Mimi nakupenda."

"Techihhila."

"Nanun tongshinun sarang hamnida."

Recognize any of these? They all say the same thing in French, German, Italian, Swahili, Sioux, and Korean. They are the most important words you would want to speak if you were going to speak sweeter and you had a limited amount of time to do it. You know what they are. They are the words, "I love you" — the most important words in any language, and yet sometimes, the hardest to say.

In our family, when we say our goodbyes over the phone to each other we always say, "I love you." It's standard procedure and sometimes feels a little dorky (especially to my kids when they are around their friends) but if you knew your condition was terminal you would not want to shortchange anyone from even one expression of love.

I just spoke today with a friend recovering from open-heart surgery. I wouldn't call him a really close friend necessarily, but at the end of the conversation

41

I had the strongest urge to tell him I loved him. Now I wouldn't normally do that at this stage in a relationship, but it was his physical fragility and proximity to death that brought it out. I'm pretty sure I was saying: "Hey, I'm just starting to really like you, and I almost lost you. We're going to spend eternity together, but not so darn fast!" I'm not sure I completely know why, but when life is precious, love is easier to express.

Romans 12:9-10 (NLT) says, *"Don't just pretend that you love others. Really love them. Hate what is wrong. Stand on the side of the good. Love each other with genuine affection, and take delight in honoring each other."*

Love is always a big part of any equation in the Body of Christ. Here Paul challenges us to love with genuine affection. And I believe we are speaking here of love both lived out and spoken.

Some may be quick to point out that love only spoken falls short of love acted out, but neither one of these should be taken at the expense of the other. We all need verbal reaffirmation of love. You can't just know you are loved. You can't run year after year on the unspoken assumption that someone loves you. We need to hear it. We hear it from the Word of God over and over and we can never get enough. We need to hear it from each other as well.

A good idea would be to say, "I love you," when it's not expected. Our family habit of saying "I love you" when we hang up the phone is fine, but an "I love you" in the middle of the day or the middle of a sentence shows that you are actually thinking about your love for someone. It's not just a habit. It's a real expression from the heart. God knows we all need that, in any language.

Response

1. What are some of the barriers you have to verbalizing your love? What can you do to overcome those barriers?

2. How many times a day do you say "I love you" in your family? Increase that number today!

3. Think about how you can speak your love in more unexpected ways. How can you remind yourself to do this?

Roses On Wednesday
Week 3: Day 3

The first roses came on a Wednesday when Horton came back into Edna's life after leaving for a season. He showed up at her doorstep with a dozen roses and his issues resolved, and in her words, "We embraced, and it was all over."

So began the story of a remarkable marriage — average perhaps to most who knew them casually, but remarkable to anyone privileged to get a closer look. For what one found on the inside observing this couple even after 40+ years of marriage was a man supremely delighted with his wife, and a woman supremely happy in the love of her husband. Had this couple found out they had only one more day together, I honestly don't think much would have changed because they were already living love for each other to the limit.

When I asked Horton if there was a secret to their relationship, he told me the story that has come to be known in my house as "Roses on Wednesday." You see the roses weren't only for that first Wednesday. They would continue to come every Wednesday for the rest of their lives together.

When it became clear that there was something special about Wednesdays, Edna asked him why. He told her that Wednesday with her was not just a day to get you one day closer to the weekend; it was simply, a phenomenal day.

King Solomon gave us a similar piece of advice. *"Let your wife be a fountain of blessing for you. Rejoice in the wife of your youth"* (Proverbs 5:18 NLT).

Horton's secret was to take an ordinary day and use it to express extraordinary love. And, likewise, Proverbs 5 says that we husbands have a choice to see and treat our wives as a fountain of blessing. Regardless of the circumstances, I can choose to rejoice in the wife of my youth.

Husbands, remember when you first laid eyes on your wife—how beautiful she was? It started with us, and so it continues. Happy wives have husbands who keep seeing them as beautiful. And one tangible way to communicate that is to make Wednesday a phenomenal day. It doesn't have to be a dozen roses. One works just as well. And if roses don't work for you, find out what does. Vary it from week to week. Believe me, it's a simple gesture with magical results.

And for those of you who aren't married, keep this as an example for when you are. And in the meantime, do something thoughtful and extraordinary for someone you love. Don't be afraid to be extravagant. After all, you never know when will be your last opportunity to bring roses on Wednesday.

Follow Horton's example and you will already be living like you were dying, because you will be demonstrating your love on a regular basis.

Response

1. When did someone surprise you with extraordinary and extravagant love?

2. Okay guys, here's the truth: If you want to take this on as a habit, it doesn't matter that everyone in your church, including your wife, has now been exposed to this concept. She will still see what you do as something special, unique and full of surprise. Guaranteed. So get creative. Then, pick your day and method... and just do it.

For motivation, check out the free download of John Fischer's song, "Roses On Wednesday" at www.fischtank.com.

Risky Love
Week 3; Day 4

She would go to church if she felt like she would be accepted, but her sense of shame keeps her back. She's gotten as close as the parking lot, but cannot gather enough courage to get out of her car. How will she explain this aborted trip to three anxious kids after talking them into coming? She doesn't know, but she decides that will be easier than explaining why she doesn't have a husband to all those happy Christian families she supposes are inside.

Then the memories of the church women's retreat someone convinced her to attend come rushing back to her. All of the teaching and discussion had been about marriage. Most of the jokes were about everyone's husbands stuck at home with the kids. She did not find this funny. She would have taken any of their husbands for even a day of relief and role modeling for her fatherless sons. A new relationship with one of these women would have made the weekend worthwhile, but no one sought her out or made any attempt to follow up. They were all too caught up in the similarities of their own lives and shared experiences.

Unfortunately, this is a scene played out in all too many churches that have not learned how to care for those at risk in their body. Jesus said, *"If you love only those who love you, what good is that?*

Even corrupt tax collectors do that much. If you are kind only to your friends, how are you different from anyone else? Even pagans do that." (Matthew 5:46-47 NLT)

Or to put it another way: If you only love those who are just like you, you are acting like a country club and not a church.

One of the surest ways love can be recognized in the body of Christ is the degree to which love is extended towards those who may not be able to give anything back, at least not right away. Many of these people stay away due to guilt and a sense of condemnation. The initial challenge is to help them know they are welcome.

One way to do this is through acts of kindness or love in action, such as advertising free services to single moms (or whatever group you might agree to target) — car tune-ups, house repair, yard work, baby-sitting — no questions asked. It's all about being sensitive to those outside our norm. We picked single moms so we could go a little deeper with this, but the same applies to pregnant girls, the physically and mentally challenged, kids on drugs, single dads, seniors living alone, recovering addicts, and the list goes on. This is both risky love (outside of our comfort zone) and loving those at risk. The hope is that new and accepting relationships can naturally flow out of these acts of kindness so that some of these people will get farther than just the parking lot.

It's time to love deeper. That deeper love will be risky, but only then will it get beyond what tax collectors and pagans do.

Response

1. Reread paragraph 2. To what extent can we create pain in others without even noticing it? How can we become more sensitive to those with different life experiences than our own?

2. Come up with a game plan to put love into action. How can you enlist the support of others in the church to do this? Be sure you treat those you reach out to with dignity. One of the best ways to do this is to listen to their story. Make sure they feel like a friend with something to offer. The last thing anyone needs is to be patronized.

Overcoming Love
Week 3; Day 5

"The end of all things is near. Therefore be clear minded and self-controlled so that you can pray. Above all, love each other deeply, because love covers over a multitude of sins." (1 Peter 4:7-8)

I bet you didn't know that Peter told us to live like we were dying. Here is what he said about it:

Because the end of all things is near,

1. Be ready to pray,

2. Love deeper, and

3. Love in such a way as to overcome the barriers to love.

Sound familiar? Peter would have liked the "Live Like You Were Dying" song. It has all the elements he felt were important to focus on with limited time left.

Are you surprised he put prayer at the top? If you knew the end was near, prayer would seem like a natural thing. You would want to get connected with where you were going. Prayer is eternal. So daily be in a spirit where prayer is a breath away.

And you would want to love those around you deeply, because love gives life meaning and connects you to those who are most precious to you. Love is of God and lasts forever. When we get to heaven we will love everybody, so we might as well get started now.

You would also want to love because love overcomes the barriers that keep us from each other. It covers over a multitude of sins.

Sin separates us — our sins against others, their sins against us. We let each other down. We belittle, judge, gossip, and otherwise destroy one another. But love is so powerful; it can overcome all of that. It covers it over. It buries it. This is not even forgiveness. It is God's love working through us — a love so great that it can overlook offenses.

There are a lot of things that love does. 1 Corinthians 13 lists many outward expressions. Peter has chosen one aspect of love particularly applicable to the shortness of time. When time is short, you want to set things straight. You don't want to leave this life with unresolved hatred in your heart towards somebody. When my father died, he had everything already taken care of right down to the flowers on the casket. He was meticulous about this. He made sure all his affairs were in order.

In the same way, when you live like you were dying, you want to have all your relationships straightened out and in order, at least on your end. We have no control over how others feel about us, but we can love them, and do so enough to absorb however they have harmed or offended us. Love makes up for all offenses.

"Hatred stirs up dissension, but love covers over all wrongs." (Proverbs 10:12)

Response

1. Is there a relationship where you need to apply this kind of love? Is there any reason why you can't love this way? Ask God to help you. He is the author of this love.

2. Covering over wrongs done to us means we have to let go of them. This can be difficult because it means letting go of our pride, but we need to do it. Pray for God's ability to truly forgive those who have wronged you.

3. Spend a few moments right now thanking God that his love has covered over all your sins.

No Record of Wrongs
Week 4; Day 1

"...and I gave forgiveness I'd been denying." Those seven words from the song "Live Like You Were Dying" are definitely worth pondering.

What causes us to deny forgiveness?

Revenge. When you have been hurt deeply, the natural human response is to want the person who hurt you to go through an equal amount of suffering. Even the Old Testament law calls for an eye for an eye and a tooth for a tooth. It is an equal and fair form of justice, but God's grace works on a different basis entirely. Grace refuses to seek revenge and it forgives. Jesus modeled this for us. 1 Peter 2:23 (NLT) says, *"He did not retaliate when he was insulted. When he suffered, he did not threaten to get even. He left his case in the hands of God, who always judges fairly."*

God knows that if all of us were to receive just payment for our sins that would be the end of the human race, so he has forgiven everyone and asks us to do the same. It's a remarkable turn of events but it's the only way there will be any healing or restoration in broken relationships.

Another reason we might deny forgiveness is that we want to hang on to our hurt because it has become our identity, a ready excuse, a smoke screen that blots out other problems we don't want to face. Consider the beggar in John 5:6 who had been sitting by the healing pool for thirty-seven years when Jesus came up to him and asked him if he wanted to get well. He didn't exactly say a hearty "Yes!" Instead he went into his well-worn excuse — his catch-22 that no one was there to lift him into the pool — and skirted the question entirely. Some of us have been so identified with our anger and bitterness that we are afraid to let go and forgive. How differently we would live if we refused to use our hurt to gain attention and sympathy!

Or perhaps we deny forgiveness because we have never believed in our own forgiveness. True forgiveness begins there. If we can't forgive ourselves, we are going to find it impossible to forgive anyone else. Judgment and blame of others always grows out of unresolved guilt. Forgive yourself first by accepting your forgiveness from God, and then offer that forgiveness to others.

Living like you were dying cuts through all of these diversions. It's pointless to go to the grave with an unforgiving heart. Dying puts a real crimp in anyone's plans for retribution! Like the cartoon of a gravestone that reads: "Now will you finally believe I was really sick?" there's just no benefit for the dead! You might as well forgive now.

One of the definitions of love in 1 Corinthians 13:5 is that *"[love] keeps no record of wrongs."* It's that simple. Ask God to give you short-term memory loss when it comes to people who have wronged you.

It's the only way to break the cycle of retribution that causes wars in our relationships. Start by receiving your own forgiveness from God. Then settle the issue once and for all against those who have harmed you by forgiving them first in your heart and then, if possible, to their face. Stop being a scorekeeper and throw away your scorecard. An unforgiving heart is an unnecessary tragedy that only hurts the one who possesses it. You have precious little time left. Just let it go.

Response

1. Is there something in your life for which you are having a difficult time accepting God's forgiveness?

2. Search your soul and see if there are any grudges toward someone deep in your heart. You may need to spend some time doing this because we train ourselves not to see these things and allow them to eat at us slowly. Ask your closest friend, spouse, or children who they think you need to forgive.

3. If you are holding a grudge against someone, forgive that person in your heart right now — don't wait another second. God is ready to embrace you in this courageous step. You are not alone. Now make a plan to extend that forgiveness face-to-face if necessary.

Why Not Forgive?
Week 4; Day 2

What do we think we are gaining by not forgiving someone? Have you ever thought about that? Being unforgiving is something of which we're not very conscious; it's a natural human reaction to being hurt. That's probably because, if we actually thought through what we were doing, we would see how useless it is. However, today let's think about it.

The main reason we withhold forgiveness is most often a desire for justice, which isn't entirely wrong. Justice is good and right, but not in our hands. Only God can judge fairly and impartially. Yet someone needs to pay for wrongs done, and we think that by not forgiving someone we are evening the score. If someone has hurt us, we believe our refusal to forgive is a way of hurting that person back — letting the offender know just how serious an offense they have committed. We might even think we are giving God a helping hand with justice. To forgive would be to "let them off the hook," when what we really want to do is inflict upon them something of the pain they have caused us.

But think a little further about this. What do we actually accomplish by refusing to forgive? Usually not what we seek. Payment extracted is rarely equal to the crime. We damage ourselves far more in this process than we do anyone else. We think we are making a big impact by not forgiving someone when, in fact, we are only carrying on our own private vendetta in our heads. Hold a grudge and so what? Everyone's lives move on — everyone, that is except our own. That is how it goes when we deny forgiveness: we try to punish someone, but in reality, we are the ones who remain in prison.

If justice is the big deal (and it is) we are not good disseminators of it. Here's what the Bible says about this: *"Do not repay anyone evil for evil. Be careful to do what is right in the eyes of everybody. If it is possible, as far as it depends on you, live at peace with everyone. Do not take revenge, my friends, but leave room for God's wrath, for it is written: 'It is mine to avenge; I will repay,' says the Lord"* (Romans 12:17-19).

Justice will be done, but not by our hand. In fact, we don't want to have anything to do with this business, because if we do, we are placing ourselves under God's judgment as well.

Which do you want for yourself: God's justice, or God's mercy? I can't think, given this choice, why anyone in his right mind would choose God's justice; and yet, when we judge someone else, that is what we are doing. We are announcing to God that we are choosing justice over mercy.

On the other hand, if we want mercy, then that is what we must give. We can't have it both ways. We can't have mercy for ourselves, and justice for all the people we don't like.

So "as far as it depends on you, live at peace with everyone."

Response

1. Think about a time when you were denying forgiveness to someone. Sometimes unforgiveness disguises itself. Search your heart. Is there bitterness, cynicism, or distrust? Seriously consider this question, "How has my lack of forgiveness impacted my life?"

2. This week, be a peacemaker. Don't be so easily offended. Don't cling so tightly to your rights. Be a little more understanding and see if anyone notices.

The Power of Forgiveness
Week 4; Day 3

"Father, forgive them, for they do not know what they are doing" (Luke 23:34).

These familiar words of Christ were uttered from the cross about the people who were in the act of crucifying him on false charges. It's hard to imagine a more demanding circumstance for forgiveness to be offered. It is the ultimate example of forgiveness, and it was extended to us in that we all participated in his death via our sins. It is a high standard indeed that Christ set.

A current expression of unusual forgiveness from a human standpoint was set in motion on April 16, 2007, when a twenty-three-year-old Virginia Tech student coldly and methodically took the lives of thirty-two of his classmates before turning the gun on himself and ending his own lonely, tragic life. As the events were reported and interpreted, conflicting opinions surfaced about how many died that day. Was it thirty-two, or thirty-three? Those who say thirty-two refuse to place any value on the life of someone who would do such a thing. He was an animal or a demon — short of being human — and unworthy of being given the same value as the lives he took. Those who say thirty-three saw the shooter as a person with value as well, a deeply disturbed person with no friends but still created in the image of God.

The difference between these views has huge implications on forgiveness.

An alumnus of Virginia Tech reported it was clear that those who planned an on-campus memorial to the victims intended to mourn the death of thirty-three people by putting out as many stones in memory of each life.

"Memorabilia was left at each stone for the respective persons," he wrote, "even the shooter. So many artifacts were left at each stone that most of it has been moved inside. There was a table for each of those killed including Seung-Hui Cho, the shooter. On his table one item that touched me was a simple 3 x 5 card with the words 'I forgive you' on it and no signature — almost as if God had left it there for him. His table was full of as many artifacts as anyone, most of which reflected this feeling of forgiveness."

This is an extraordinary inclusion. Those who advocate such quick forgiveness must know that the alternative is to seethe with anger, resentment, and bitterness that can eat away a person's insides and render one incapable of kindness or grace. To refuse to give forgiveness is to become, yourself, a victim of another's crime. Those who refuse to forgive the shooter are perpetuating the control of his act over them. By forgiving, you take away that person's power over you. You turn things back over to God and trust him for justice to be done more wisely than you or I could ever determine it. There is no healing of wrongs done to us apart from forgiveness.

If Christ can forgive all of us for crucifying him with our sins, what crime is so great that we can't forgive someone who has sinned against us (a sin already forgiven by the cross)?

"Instead, be kind to each other, tenderhearted, forgiving one another, just as God through Christ has forgiven you." (Ephesians 4:32 NLT)

Response

1. Read carefully the account of Jesus' death in Luke 23:26-49. Reflect on what Christ had to endure so you could be forgiven.

2. What can you learn from these students at Virginia Tech that is applicable to your life?

Making Peace
Week 4; Day 4

Funeral and memorial services are sometimes tough on family members. At a loved one's death, we rejoice in the hope of heaven, but we also feel our own mortality more than ever.

We wonder if we have sufficiently said our peace. Have grudges been resolved and disappointments been forgiven? Could we have done something to shave the distance that still existed between us? A helplessness sets in as the end nears.

But there is also a warm, enveloping blanket of God's grace over this all. We feel our own mortality, see someone else's, and yet somehow there is an ability to accept, as the Serenity Prayer has it, "what we cannot change."

The only regret we may have is: Why didn't we come to this realization sooner? Why do we have to be near the end before we can let go? We apply God's grace and forgiveness at the end because we don't have a choice; we need to learn how to do this while we do have a choice.

Forgiveness is all about letting go. Those who don't forgive are the ones who find themselves mired in their own hostility and blame, headed toward becoming the very thing they hate. We think we are setting the other person free by forgiving, but we are really doing ourselves the biggest favor. Forgiveness becomes for us a sigh of relief — a newfound freedom.

The Serenity Prayer, by Reinhold Niebuhr, and popularized through the Alcoholics Anonymous movement, is a fitting prayer for living like you were dying.

> God grant me the serenity
> To accept the things I cannot change;
> Courage to change the things I can;
> And wisdom to know the difference.

Part of what we cannot change is what others have done to us. Part of what we can change is to forgive them and release them from our judgment. It takes courage, but we have to forgive in order to be at peace with others and ourselves. We can forgive. We can let it go. And the sooner we do this, the better. Don't wait until someone's deathbed, or your own.

Many people do not realize that the Serenity Prayer doesn't end there. The rest of this prayer may not be as well known as the first four lines, but it is well suited for our study.

> Living one day at a time;
> Enjoying one moment at a time;
> Accepting hardships as the pathway to peace;
> Taking, as He did, this sinful world
> As it is, not as I would have it;

Trusting that He will make all things right
If I surrender to His Will;
That I may be reasonably happy in this life
And supremely happy with Him
Forever in the next.
Amen.

This is the essence of forgiveness: surrender of our expectations, our rights, and our pride to God's will; giving him control in our lives and trusting that he has our best in mind in all circumstances.

Some of you are trapped in the hold of a particularly helpless form of unforgiveness, because the person you are unwilling to forgive is no longer alive. You can't find peace, because you can't go to them, nor can they release you. But God can release you, in fact, he already has. All that remains is for you to believe him and let go. So let it go, and step into the freedom of God's forgiveness, both for you and for the person you need to forgive. It's your choice now.

Response

1. When was the last time you lost a relative, friend, or neighbor? Were you on good terms? Were you close? Could you have been closer? What were your regrets? Now take those regrets and apply the lesson learned to someone who is alive. Determine a plan of action for that person.

2. Is there someone with whom you are having a conflict? If that person were dying, would you go to them? What would you say?

3. Are you unable to forgive someone who has passed on? Even though they are gone, it can be helpful to write that person a letter, and set them and yourself free.

Living Like You Were Dying
Week 4; Day 5

As we come to the end of this 30-day journey, we conclude with some thoughts from a young man whose life, even at only twenty years, resonates with the source of our study.

Michael Simon believes that the song, "Live Like You Were Dying" is sort of a theme song for him. "I grab life by the horns and don't let go — seizing the day and squeezing the life out of it for all it is worth. Because of my mother's nine-year battle with breast cancer, I don't really take time for granted. I don't leave questions unasked and don't hesitate to express love in any form."

Here is a young man who has lived for the last nine years considering each day in the company of his mother to be his last. Three things he brings up here are significant conclusions for our study.

1. Make the most of every moment. It may be the last.

As we have seen, time is a precious commodity. Michael realizes that and spends it wisely and passionately. He is acutely aware of time passing, and each new day he has with his mother is a blessing. And this has been going on for nine years! His example gives a realistic picture of what living like you were dying can actually do for you. It puts you in a state of suspended animation that forces you to not take anything for granted but to be thankful in all things. It is like a "time alert" that steps up all areas of alertness.

Jesus spoke of this mindset in Mark 13:33 when he said of his return: *"Be on guard! Be alert! You do not know when that time will come."* He is telling us to live each day as if it were our last.

2. Live with no regrets — no unfinished business.

"Brothers, I do not consider myself yet to have taken hold of it. But one thing I do: Forgetting what is behind and straining toward what is ahead, I press on toward the goal to win the prize for which God has called me heavenward in Christ Jesus." (Philippians 3:13-14)

Michael doesn't look back. What has happened has happened. He is more concerned with discovering the "what now's" of the present and the future than he is the "why's" of the past. He doesn't leave anything unasked, and I have a feeling he's not waiting around for the answer, either. Answers come to those who seek. Michael has no regrets because he knows everything that happens, happens for a reason, and his life is all about wrestling those reasons out of his experiences.

3. Love with urgency.

Michael doesn't hesitate to express love in any form. I would take this to mean that he shares his love for his mom in words, in deeds, in remembering what is important to her, in sending her notes and reminders of his love, in listening when she needs to talk, and being silent when the last thing she needs is someone giving her advice. Maybe he takes her to places she loves where she can do what she loves to do.

And here's the final word and it's very important. Michael lives this way in relation to his mother, but everyone else in his life gets the benefit, because this intensity spills over into all of his other relationships and responsibilities as well. Because of her, he takes nothing for granted. Can you say the same?

Response

1. What have you learned as a result of this study? How would you like to live differently as a result of these last thirty days?

2. As we conclude this study, ask God to put you on a time alert — to view life in slow motion so as to appreciate every moment for what it is.

3. Commit yourself to continuing to meet with your group or even one other person weekly to remind each another to live like you were dying. It's only as you actually face this possibility together that you can benefit from its perspective.

SMALL GROUP SESSIONS | SESSION 1
LIVE LIKE YOU WERE DYING

With Presenter Gary Smalley

Get Started

If you are a new group, spend some time getting to know each other.

1. Suppose you only had thirty days left to live and you could take one final trip anywhere in the world, where would you go?

2. If you had one month left to live, what would you do that you've never done before?

3. Before you start the video, take a few moments to pray. Ask God to meet with you and give you open minds and hearts.

Watch The video

Key Verse
for the Week

Teach us to make the
most of our time, so
that we may grow in
wisdom.

Psalm 90:12 (NLT)

Talk It Over

1. What is the closest you have ever come to death? Was it a friend or family member? Perhaps you have had a near death experience yourself. How did that experience impact you?

2. If you had been lying on the ground waiting for the paramedics, what would have been going through your mind?

3. In his hunting story, Gary referenced this week's key verse, Psalm 90:12, which says *"Teach us to make the most of our time, so that we may grow in wisdom."* How would you define wisdom? What is the correlation between making the most of our time and growing in wisdom?

4. As Gary got his second chance at life, he began to re-prioritize. He asked, "God, what do you consider the greatest things on this earth?" Jesus clearly and definitively answered that question in Matthew 22.

"Jesus replied 'You must love the Lord your God with all your heart, all your soul, and all your mind.' This is the first and greatest commandment. A second is equally important: 'Love your neighbor as yourself.' All the other commandments and all the demands of the prophets are based on these two commandments."

Matthew 22:37–40 (NLT)

What does it look like for you to really love God and make him your highest priority? If you had a second chance at life, what changes would you make to love God with your whole heart?

5. One of the results of Gary's close encounter with death was a fresh hunger for God and his Word. King David in the Old Testament described a similar hunger for God.

O God, you are my God;
    I earnestly search for you.
My soul thirsts for you;
    my whole body longs for you
in this parched and weary land
    where there is no water.
I have seen you in your sanctuary
    and gazed upon your power and glory.
Your unfailing love is better to me than life itself;
        how I praise you!
I will honor you as long as I live,
    lifting up my hands to you in prayer.
You satisfy me more than the richest of foods.
    I will praise you with songs of joy.
I lie awake thinking of you,
    meditating on you through the night.
I think how much you have helped me;
    I sing for joy in the shadow of your protecting wings.
I follow close behind you;
    your strong right hand holds me securely.

Psalm 63:1-8 (NLT)

Describe a time in your life when you were most hungry to know and experience God. What is your greatest roadblock to pursuing God passionately?

6. Gary closed this session with three things he focuses on each day to help him live out the Great Commandment of loving God and loving people. What practical steps can you take each day to fuel your "hunger for God"?

Live It Out

Here are 3 steps you could use to start your day:

1. Admit you are a beggar. Acknowledge that you can do nothing of worth without God.

2. Acknowledge God as the king (CEO) of your life. Embrace the truth that he is the master of your life and big enough to handle any and every need.

3. Ask for the Holy Spirit's help and power. Throughout your day, call on the Holy Spirit to guide you.

Start by doing these three things. Write them out on a 3x5 card and begin each day by putting them into action.

Scripture Citations used in Session 1

Listed below are the Scripture verses Gary used during Session One of the teaching video. Commit these verses to memory and use them to transform your life in ways that will let you live like you were dying.

Love the Lord your God with all your heart and with all your soul and with all your mind.

Matthew 22:37

Love your neighbor as yourself.

Matthew 22:39

The entire law is summed up in a single command: "love your neighbor as yourself."

Galatians 5:14

I have hidden your word in my heart that I might not sin again you.

Psalm 119:11

Blessed are the poor in spirit, for theirs is the kingdom of heaven.

Matthew 5:3

For the kingdom of God is not a matter of eating and drinking, but of righteousness, peace and joy in the Holy Spirit.

Romans 14:17

SMALL GROUP SESSIONS | SESSION 2
SPEAK SWEETLY

With Presenter Gary Smalley

Get Started

Describe a funny experience when you said something you wished you hadn't.

Watch The Video

Talk It Over

1. As you think back over your life, who has affirmed or encouraged you in such a way that it still has an impact on you to this day?

2. Matthew 12:34 (NLT) says *"… For whatever is in your heart determines what you say."* Matthew 15:18 (NLT) says *"But evil words come from an evil heart and defile the person who says them."*

Gary emphasized that the words we speak can be traced back to what's in our heart. What are some things people feed on with their mind, eyes, and heart that negatively impact their words? What spiritual things can you feed on that will positively impact your words?

Food for Thought: Do a little self-assessment. If someone followed you around this week and listened to your conversations, how would they describe you…encouraging? complaining? negative? optimistic? kind? impatient?

Key Verse for this week

So encourage each other and build each other up, just as you are already doing.

1 Thessalonians 5:11 (NLT)

3. Proverbs 18:21 says *"The tongue has the power of life and death, and those who love it will eat its fruit."* Speaking of the tongue, James 3:9-10 (NLT) says *"Sometimes it praises our Lord and Father, and sometimes it breaks out into curses against those who have been made in the image of God. ¹⁰And so blessing and cursing come pouring out of the same mouth. Surely, my brothers and sisters, this is not right!"*

Small words can have huge impact. In what relationship or area of your life do you find it most difficult to "speak sweeter"? How can you speak blessing into that situation this week? Will you?

4. Read the four verses that Gary talked about. He described these verses as seeds in his own life which changed his beliefs and ultimately changed his words.

We can rejoice, too, when we run into problems and trials, for we know that they are good for us — they help us learn to endure. And endurance develops strength of character in us, and character strengthens our confident expectation of salvation. And this expectation will not disappoint us. For we know how dearly God loves us, because he has given us the Holy Spirit to fill our hearts with his love.

Romans 5:3–5 (NLT)

No matter what happens, always be thankful, for this is God's will for you who belong to Christ Jesus.

1 Thessalonians 5:18 (NLT)

Each time he said, "My gracious favor is all you need. My power works best in your weakness." So now I am glad to boast about my weaknesses, so that the power of Christ may work through me. Since I know it is all for Christ's good, I am quite content with my weaknesses and with insults, hardships, persecutions, and calamities. For when I am weak, then I am strong.

2 Corinthians 12:9–10 (NLT)

And we know that God causes everything to work together for the good of those who love God and are called according to his purpose for them.

Romans 8:28 (NLT)

These are God's words of encouragement to us as he "speaks sweetly" to us. Share which of these passages most encourages you today?

5. Consider the following "sweet words." Which of these words or phrases can you focus on this week?

- Thank you
- Please
- I love you
- I appreciate you
- I'm praying for you
- You mean a lot to me
- Thanks for your friendship
- I'm glad you are in my life

Live It Out

Write down the names of four or five people who need sweeter words from you. Pray for each of them this week and find ways to bless them with your words.

- _____
- _____
- _____
- _____
- _____

Parent Opportunity: Write a letter of blessing to each of your children this week. This could be something they will treasure for their whole life.

If you aren't married or don't have children, write a letter of blessing to your parents, a sibling, your spouse, or a best friend or person of significance in your life.

Scripture Citations used in Session 2

Listed below are the Scripture verses Gary used during Session Two of the teaching video. Commit these verses to memory and use them to transform your life in ways that will let you live like you were dying.

When your words came, I ate them; they were my joy and my heart's delight, for I bear your name, O Lord God Almighty.

Jeremiah 15:16

Not only so, but we also rejoice in our sufferings, because we know that suffering produces perseverance; perseverance, character; and character, hope. And hope does not disappoint us, because God has poured out his love into our hearts by the Holy Spirit, whom he has given us.

Romans 5:3-5

Give thanks in all circumstances, for this is God's will for you in Christ Jesus.

1 Thessalonians 5:18

But he said to me, "My grace is sufficient for you, for my power is made perfect in weakness." Therefore I will boast all the more gladly about my weaknesses, so that Christ's power may rest on me. That is why, for Christ's sake, I delight in weaknesses, in insults, in hardships, in persecution, in difficulties. For when I am weak, then I am strong.

2 Corinthians 12:9-10

And we know that in all things God works for the good of those who love him, who have been called according to his purpose.

Romans 8:28

SMALL GROUP SESSIONS | SESSION 3
LOVE DEEPER

With Presenter Gary Smalley

Get Started

Brainstorm as a group and make a list of all the songs you know that have the word "love" in the title?

Describe the first time you were ever "smitten" by love.

Watch the Video

Talk It Over

1. What is the most extravagant expression of love you've ever received?

2. What biblical examples can you think of where extravagant love was expressed?

3. Read slowly these words about God's extravagant love toward us.

   "But then God our Savior showed us his kindness and love. He saved us, not because of the good things we did, but because of his mercy. He washed away our sins and gave us a new life through the Holy Spirit. He generously poured out the Spirit upon us because of what Jesus Christ our Savior did. He declared us not guilty because of his great kindness. And now we know that we will inherit eternal life."

   Titus 3:4-7 (NLT)

Key Verse
for the week

For the whole law can be summed up in one command: "Love your neighbor as yourself."

Galatians. 5:14 (NLT)

84

Have someone in the group share briefly how they became a Christian and how the love of Christ has changed them. Then consider taking a few moments as a group to pray and praise God for his deep and extravagant love.

4. Gary referenced Galatians 5:14 (NLT) which says, *"For the whole law can be summed up in this one command: 'Love your neighbor as yourself.'"*

One day Jesus had an encounter with a man who was a religious expert and Jesus was asked the question "who is my neighbor?" Read Jesus' answer in Luke 10:30–37 (NLT).

Jesus replied with an illustration: "A Jewish man was traveling on a trip from Jerusalem to Jericho, and he was attacked by bandits. They stripped him of his clothes and money, beat him up, and left him half dead beside the road. By chance a Jewish priest came along; but when he saw the man lying there, he crossed to the other side of the road and passed him by. A Temple assistant walked over and looked at him lying there, but he also passed by on the other side. Then a despised Samaritan came along, and when he saw the man, he felt deep pity. Kneeling beside him, the Samaritan soothed his wounds with medicine and bandaged them. Then he put the man on his own donkey and took him to an inn, where he took care of him. The next day he handed the innkeeper two pieces of silver and told him to take care of the man. 'If his bill runs higher than that,' he said, 'I'll pay the difference the next time I am here.' Now which of these three would you say was a neighbor to the man who was attacked by bandits?" Jesus asked. The man replied, "The one who showed him mercy." Then Jesus said, "Yes, now go and do the same."

Make a list of the ways the Samaritan showed love.

- _____

- _____

- _____

- _____

- _____

5. Who are you not noticing that needs to be shown love? To whom could you express generous love? What are some ways you could be a "Good Samaritan" in their life?

6. If you knew you had only days to live, who would need to hear "I love you" from your lips?

   What would hold you back from saying those three simple, but powerful words? Is it hurry? awkwardness? fear of rejection? past hurt?

Live It Out

Choose something you could do as a group that would be an "over the top," extravagant expression of love. Who in your church or community could be blessed with this generous love?

Look for every opportunity possible this week to say "I love you." Go for it.

Scripture Citations used in Session 3

Listed below are the Scripture verses Gary used during Session Three of the teaching video. Commit these verses to memory and use them to transform your life in ways that will let you live like you were dying.

> *You, my brothers, were called to be free. But do not use your freedom to indulge the sinful nature; rather, serve one another in love. The entire law is summed up in a single command: "love your neighbor as yourself." If you keep on biting and devouring each other, watch out or you will be destroyed by each other.*
>
> Galatians 5:13–15

> *Blessed are the poor in spirit, for theirs is the kingdom of heaven.*
>
> Matthew 5:3

> *But he gives us more grace. That is why Scripture says, "God opposes the proud but gives grace to the humble."*
>
> James 4:6

Notes

SMALL GROUP SESSIONS | SESSION 4
GIVE FORGIVENESS

With Presenter Gary Smalley

Remember the Lord forgave you

Get Started

Name one thing you've always wanted to do, but have never gotten around to?

Watch the Video

Talk It Over

1. What did Gary say in this week's session that grabbed you the most?

2. Think back to a time when somebody forgave you and let you off the hook. What emotions did you experience? What has happened to the relationship since then?

3. Colossians 3:12–13 (NLT) says *"Since God chose you to be the holy people whom he loves, you must clothe yourselves with tenderhearted mercy, kindness, humility, gentleness, and patience. You must make allowance for each other's faults and forgive the person who offends you. Remember, the Lord forgave you, so you must forgive others."*

Discuss some practical ways that you can "make allowance for each other's faults."

Key Verse
for this Week

...Remember, the Lord forgave you, so you must forgive others.

Colossians 3:13b (NLT)

4. Gary said that unforgiveness is like drinking poison and hoping the other person gets sick. Ephesians 4:31–32 (NLT) says, *"Get rid of all bitterness, rage, anger, harsh words, and slander, as well as all types of malicious behavior. Instead, be kind to each other, tenderhearted, forgiving one another, just as God through Christ has forgiven you."*

Which of the words in verse 31 jumps out at you as the poison you most need to beware of? What is the antidote described in verse 32?

5. Who have you been denying forgiveness and what is keeping you from giving forgiveness? To help you really discover the answer, here are some additional questions to ponder.

- Who would your wife, kids, and best friends say that you need to forgive?

- Who do you feel anger and resentment toward when their name comes up?

- Who are you talking about more than you are talking to?

- When the topic of forgiveness comes up, whose name immediately pops into your mind?

Live It Out

1. As a group, pray together for those needing to reconcile relationships. Ask the Lord to direct you in the timing and approach to conversations that need to take place.

2. Do a spiritual inventory of the broken relationships in your

life. From whom do you need to ask for forgiveness? To whom do you need to offer forgiveness?

3. Call, e-mail, or text message—do something to reach out to the people you need to reconcile with. Ask the group to hold you accountable to this.

Scripture Citations used in Session 4

Listed below are the Scripture verses Gary used during Session Four of the teaching video. Commit these verses to memory and use them to transform your life in ways that will let you live like you were dying.

Yet I am writing you a new command; its truth is seen in him and you, because the darkness is passing and the true light is already shining. Anyone who claims to be in the light but hates his brother is still in the darkness. Whoever loves his brother lives in the light, and there is nothing in him to make him stumble.

1 John 2:8–10

Then you will know the truth, and the truth will set you free.

John 8:32

LIVE LIKE YOU WERE DYING
APPENDIX

HOST TIPS AND GROUP TOOLS

In this section, we will walk you through each segment of a typical ninety-minute group meeting and provide some tips to help you facilitate each part of your time together.

Before The Group Arrives

Watch the Host Coaching Tips on the teaching video. This 3-5 minute segment preceding each lesson is just for you. You will be given specific coaching tips for facilitating that lesson.

2. **Preview the DVD teaching and discussion questions.** Preview both the DVD teaching by Gary Smalley and the discussion questions. Write down any other follow-up questions that might be helpful in the group discussion.

3. **Pray for your group members by name.** Ask God to use your time together to touch the heart of every person in your group. Expect God to lead you to whomever he wants you to encourage or challenge in a special way. If you listen, God will surely lead.

4. **Provide refreshments.** There's nothing like food to help a group connect. We suggest you prepare a snack for the first week, but after that, ask other group members to bring the food and drinks so that they share in the responsibilities of the group and make a commitment to return. You can serve refreshments before or after your study; either way works great.

5. **Childcare arrangements.** If the people you invite need assistance with childcare, you could meet in one part of your home and share the cost of one or two babysitters who watch the children in another part of the home. You could also have the children cared for at a different house nearby.

6. **Relax.** Don't try to do things exactly like another host; do them in a way that fits your style and temperament. Remember that people may feel nervous just showing up at a discussion group, so put them at ease when they arrive. And don't feel like you have all the answers. Admit when you don't know something and be quick to apologize when you make a mistake. Your group will love you for it.

Getting Started

The questions in the opening section of each lesson serve three important functions:

1. They get the group talking. These questions are designed so that every person can answer them without feeling intimidated.

2. They unify the thinking. Everyone's minds will be on what was happening before they arrived, so grabbing their attention with a captivating question helps draw them into the topic.

3. They get below the surface. Sometimes answering a creative question before the teaching time helps to reveal a person's true reaction to the topic and shows them where they might benefit from the study.

Teaching Video

Watch this 10-minute teaching by Gary Smalley, and make sure everyone has a study guide in which to take notes during the session.

Talk It Over

Here are some guidelines for leading the discussion time:

- This is a discussion, not a lecture. Resist the temptation to do all the talking and answer your own questions. Don't be afraid of a few moments of silence while people formulate their answers.

- Encourage everyone to participate. Don't let one person dominate, but also don't pressure quieter members to speak during the first couple of sessions. After one person answers, don't immediately move on; ask what other people think, or say, "Would someone who hasn't shared like to add anything?"

- Affirm all answers with a "thanks" or "great answer." If an answer is clearly wrong, ask, "What led you to that conclusion?" or ask what the rest of the group thinks. If a disagreement arises, go with it! The discussion can draw out important perspectives, and if you can't resolve it there, offer to research it further and return to the issue next week.

HOST TIPS AND GROUP TOOLS

- Detour when necessary. If an important question is raised that is not in the study guide, take time to discuss it. If you have already covered a written question, skip it. Allow the Holy Spirit room to maneuver, and follow his prompting when the discussion changes direction.

- Split up into groups of 3–5 for one or more of the questions, particularly those that are more personal in nature. This is a great way to give everyone, even the quieter members, a chance to say something. Choose someone in the group to guide each of the smaller groups through the discussion. This involves others in the leadership of the group and provides an opportunity for training new leaders.

Live It Out

The simple suggestions in this section will help you apply the lesson to your life. Be sure to leave adequate time to talk about these practical applications. This is a great way to build group community. Try these ideas together and hold each other accountable for completing them, then share the following week how it went.

Plan Your Next Study

Before you finish this study, talk together about what you would like to do next. If you decide to continue meeting together, we recommend Bible studies you can do that would be a great follow-up to the topics in "Live Like You Were Dying" on our website: **www.llywd.org**

Group Roster

One of the most important things you can do in your group is to pray for each other. Record each other's concerns in the Group Prayer and Praise Records (pages 98–101), and be sure to note when God answers a prayer! Pray together for these requests—you can pray in pairs, in groups of three or four, or as a large group. If you're new to praying, it's okay to pray silently or to talk to God in a simple sentence, such as, "God, please help Laura find a job."

GROUP ROSTER

NAME	HOME PHONE	EMAIL
1.		
2.		
3.		
4.		
5.		
6.		
8.		
9.		
10.		
11.		
12.		

GROUP PRAYER AND PRAISE RECORD | SESSION 1

DATE	PERSON	PRAYER REQUEST	PRAISE REPORT

DATE	PERSON	PRAYER REQUEST	PRAISE REPORT

GROUP PRAYER AND PRAISE RECORD | **SESSION 3**

DATE	PERSON	PRAYER REQUEST	PRAISE REPORT

GROUP PRAYER AND PRAISE RECORD | **SESSION 4**

DATE	PERSON	PRAYER REQUEST	PRAISE REPORT

KEY VERSES

"I have hidden your word in my heart that I might not sin against you."

Psalm 119:11

One of the most effective ways to deepen our understanding of the principles we are learning in this series is to meditate on these key Scripture verses. Take time each week to ponder the key verse; write down your thoughts and responses to God's message to you. You may want to stretch yourself and try to memorize these verses, in which case you can use these cards to carry around with you as you work and drive and exercise.

Week One	Week Two
Teach us to make the most of our time, so that we may grow in wisdom.	*So encourage each other and build each other up, just as you are already doing.*
Psalm 90:12 (NLT)	1 Thessalonians 5:11 (NLT)
Week Three	**Week Four**
For the whole law can be summed up in this one command: *"Love your neighbor as yourself."*	*…Remember, the Lord forgave you, so you must forgive others.*
Galatians 5:14 (NLT)	Colossians 3:13b (NLT)